Lost Hong Kong

A History in Pictures

Peter Waller

UNIQUE BOOKS

Title page: In 1860, when Felice Belato took this panoramic view of the harbour, the fleets of both Britain and France were present in force prior to the outbreak of war between the two and China following the Chinese rejection of an ultimatum issued on 8 March 1860. The Anglo-French invasion of the Chinese mainland represented the final phase of the Second Opium War and resulted in the treaty that ceded the southern half of the Kowloon peninsula – south of Boundary Street – to the British. On the extreme right of the photograph can be seen the tower of St John's, the Anglican Cathedral, which was completed in 1849. To the west of the cathedral is the neo-classical building that accommodated the Central Government Offices; the foundation stone for the building was laid on 24 February 1847 and, at a cost of £14,393, the building was completed the following year. The building was to be demolished in 1954 and replacement offices were constructed on the site. To the north of the offices can be seen Johnston's House; this dated originally to the early 1840s and was one of the earliest buildings to be constructed in Hong Kong. Between 1843 and 1846 it was occupied as the residency of the Governor before a period in use as the Supreme Court. Extended in 1860, the building was used commercially, being leased to Heard & Co from the 1860s until 1876. For a brief period during the 1870s it was used as the Russian consulate. Sold in 1879 to E. R. Belilios and renamed the Beaconsfield in 1882, it was leased by the government between 1897 and 1911 before being sold in 1915 to the Missions Étrangères de Paris and demolished the following year, to be replaced by a new mission. Immediately to the north of the church can be seen the officers' mess of Murray Barracks and, beyond that structure, the North Barracks. The former was completed in 1846 and was finally demolished in 1982; the Bank of China Tower was subsequently built on the site. The North Barracks were demolished in 1960 and, between 1973 and 2018, the site was occupied by the Murray Road multi-storey car park.
Wellcome Collection

A note on the photographs
A number of the illustrations in this book have been drawn from the collection of the Online Transport Archive, a UK-registered charity that was set up to accommodate collections put together by transport enthusiasts who wished to see their precious images secured for the long-term. Further information about the archive can be found at: www.onlinetransportarchive.org or email secretary@onlinetransportarchive.org

First published in the United Kingdom by Unique Books 2019

© Text: Peter Waller 2019

© Photographs: As credited

ISBN: 978 0 9957493 5 1

A CIP record for this book is available from the British Library

Unique Books is an imprint of Unique Publishing Services Ltd, 3 Merton Court, The Strand, Brighton Marina Village, Brighton BN2 5XY.

www.uniquepublishingservices.com

Published in Hong Kong by Blacksmith Books

Unit 26, 19/F, Block B, Wah Lok Industrial Centre, 37-41 Shan Mei Street, Fo Tan, Hong Kong

www.blacksmithbooks.com

Tel: (+852) 2877 7899

ISBN: 978 988 77928 4 0

Printed in China

There are few more vibrant cities in the world than Hong Kong but one of the consequences of this is that there is almost constant change. The pressure to develop and redevelop scarce land resources has seen great areas of land reclamation on both sides of Victoria Harbour and the regular demolition and replacement of buildings. Given the nature of the terrain of Hong Kong Island, the Kowloon peninsula and the New Territories, it was inevitable that as the territory's population grew and as its economy thrived, developers would seek to exploit sites and open up new ones; not only would the area of the built environment expand exponentially but it would also stretch ever higher into the sky – a veritable Manhattan of the Far East.

The beginning was, however, relatively inauspicious and, even at the end of the 19th century, Hong Kong was relatively underdeveloped. The great trading businesses, such as Jardine Matheson & Co, were already well established and the northern shore of Hong Kong Island was witnessing the construction of prestigious and stylish buildings but it was still relatively low-key and low-rise. The first – but very limited – schemes for land reclamation had started, initiating a process that has continued for more than a century and one that is likely to continue into the future. The recent loss of both the Edinburgh Place Ferry Pier and the Queen's Pier – in 2007 and 2008 respectively – demonstrates that land reclamation schemes can and will result in changes to the built environment.

In the census of 1931 the population of Hong Kong was found to be 864,117; by 1941 when an official census was held, this had increased to 1.6 million and by 1991 to 5.75 million. In the years since then the population has increased by a further two million, totalling in excess of 7.4 million by 2017. All these people require accommodation and facilities – schools, hospitals, jobs in factories and offices, etc – and, in a region that is now the fourth most highly populated in terms of density per square kilometre, this can only be achieved by the creation of new towns – often on reclaimed land – or ever taller structures. Over the past 40 years Hong Kong has witnessed the massive growth of new settlements dominated by the ubiquitous apartment block; one example of this is Tuen Mun, which was developed initially as the Castle Peak New Town on reclaimed land from the late 1970s and which now provides accommodation for more than half a million.

The commercial heart of Hong Kong – the northern coast of Hong Kong Island itself and the southern tip of the Kowloon peninsula – has witnessed equally dramatic change; the streetscape of the late 1950s and early 1960s where many of the traditional early colonial buildings were still extant – such as the General Post Office of 1911 – was to undergo an initial transformation during the 1960s and 1970s. But even the buildings that were constructed then are now under threat, no longer deemed adequate for the bustling 21st century. In 1990 the new Bank of China Building was completed; this was – at 1,205ft in height – the first building outside the USA to exceed 1,000ft in height and was, briefly, the tallest building outside the USA in the world. Today, it's now only the fourth tallest building in Hong Kong, being dwarfed by the 1,588ft International Commerce Centre, completed in 2010, in West Kowloon and by Central Plaza and Two International Finance Centre. One of the consequences of these increasingly tall buildings is that, whilst historic buildings may survive, the skyline that overshadows them is constantly changing.

There is a recognition that historic buildings are important and between 1996 and 2000 the Antiquities & Monuments Office identified some 8,000 structures and further work between 2002 and 2004 focused on some 1,444 buildings. In 2016 there were 114 declared monuments – both man-made and natural – in the SAR along with 153 Grade I, 322 Grade II and 442 Grade III listed buildings but listing does not guarantee protection and the loss of historic structures has continued.

This book is primarily a pictorial record of buildings – largely on Hong Kong Island – and scenes that are now but memories. It cannot be comprehensive but provides a snapshot of changes wrought over more than a century. The grandeur of some of the lost buildings is remarkable but equally fascinating is – perhaps – the overall change to the skyline of both Hong Kong Island and Kowloon over a relatively short period. But perhaps the most telling view is one of the more recent: the Hau Wong Temple at Tung Chung. When recorded in 1993 it was a peaceful refuge from the bustle of the commercial centre but, in the quarter century since then, the construction of the new airport and the adjacent new town has shattered that peace.

A map of the northern part of Hong Kong Island and the southern part of the Kowloon peninsula that demonstrates the relatively sparse development of the colony in the early years of the 20th century. The Kowloon Canton Railway was formally opened through to Kowloon on 1 October 1910. The map shows also the tramway operating on Hong Kong Island; this had opened in 1904 and, when new, was largely to run on or near the coastline. Over the past century, land reclamation has seen the route of the tramway move ever further away from the harbour. *Via Commons Media*

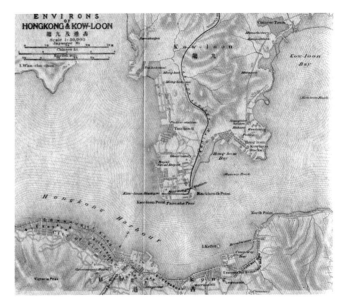

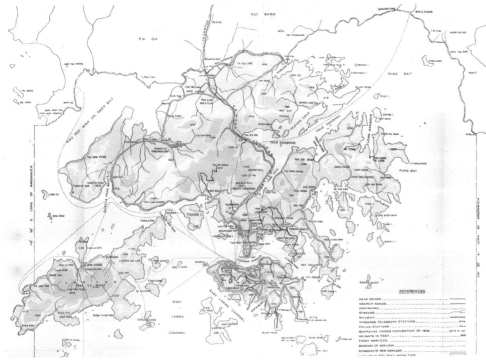

A map of Hong Kong as published in the Hong Kong government's annual report for 1947. *Author's Collection*

In 1846, less than a decade after the first British settlement on Hong Kong Island, there is already evidence of a significant community developing on the north coast of the island with a rich variety of ships – including a paddle steamer – visible in the harbour. The coastline is the original, long before the various land reclamation schemes saw the lines of the harbour radically redrawn. The original drawing for this lithograph was made by Leopold George Heath (1817-1907), who was later to be knighted. Heath was a Lieutenant aboard HMS *Iris* in 1846 when he drew this view of the island; his drawings were published in London by the Hydrographer's Office the following year as a guide to the captain of merchant ships. Heath was to have a distinguished naval career, retiring as a Vice Admiral in 1877 after a career that had extended over some 47 years.
Library of Congress

Recorded shortly after its completion in 1865 by William Pryor Floyd, Zetland Hall – nicknamed 'The Bungalow' – at the junction of Zetland Street and Ice House Street was the second Masonic Hall to serve Central, replacing an older structure. The building was designed by Charles St George Cleverly, who was the second Surveyor General in Hong Kong and the architect also of Government House. The Masonic Hall was named after the Lodge – No 525 Zetland – that commissioned it; the Lodge itself was named after Thomas Dundas, 2nd Earl of Zetland, who was Grand Master of the United Grand Lodge of England between 1844 and 1870. The building was to survive until 1944 when it was destroyed during an American raid on the territory during the Japanese occupation. A third Masonic Hall – again called Zetland Hall – was opened on Kennedy Street in 1950. The site of the second hall is now occupied by a sub-station of the Hongkong Electric Co. *Wellcome Collection*

In 1869 Prince Alfred, Duke of Edinburgh, the second son of Queen Victoria and Prince Albert, visited Hong Kong, the first member of the royal family to visit the territory. A serving officer in the Royal Navy, he travelled to Hong Kong on board HMS *Galatea*, as part of the tour that also saw him visit Sri Lanka and India. This view, recorded by the noted photographer John Thomson, records Bonham Strand decorated with mechanical figures to mark the Duke's visit. As the name implies, Bonham Strand, in Sheung Wan, originally represented a road along the shoreline; however, with the significant schemes of land reclamation, the modern Bonham Strand and Bonham Strand West are now inland. The street was named after Sir George Bonham, who, as the third Governor of Hong Kong, undertook the rebuilding of the Sheung Wan district after its destruction by fire in 1851. The Duke of Edinburgh was eventually to renounce his British titles when, in 1893, he succeeded to the title of Duke of Saxe-Coburg in Germany. He died in 1900. *Wellcome Collection*

To mark the visit of Prince Alfred to Hong Kong in 1869 a temporary triumphal arch was erected at the northern end of Pedder Street. This structure – with a view of the wharf and ships beyond – was recorded by John Thomson. Surmounting the arch is a cartouche incorporating Alfred's monogram surmounted by a ducal crown. *Wellcome Collection*

Also recorded in 1869 by John Thomson is this house on Lyndhurst Terrace again decorated to mark the visit of Prince Alfred. At the time the house was owned by members of the Parsi community, some of whom can be seen standing in front of it. Named after a British official, the street's Chinese name can be translated as Flower Arrangement Street; in the mid 19th century, Lyndhurst Terrace was the centre of the European red-light district and was lined with flower shops that sold bouquets to the customers of the local brothels. Lyndhurst Terrace, linking Pottinger Street with Hollywood Road, still exists albeit the 19th century residents would be hard pressed to recognise the narrow road today with its high-rise buildings and the Central Mid-Levels Escalator. *Wellcome Collection*

Viewed from Kellett Island with Victoria Peak in the background, this view of the harbour taken by John Thomson in about 1869 reveals a fascinating array of ships, including, closest to the camera, a two-funnel paddle steamer. Although, by this date, the Royal Navy had already introduced its first steam-powered armoured ironclad warships – HMS *Warrior* having been commissioned in 1861 – traditional warships are also prominent as is HMS *Princess Charlotte* towards the extreme right-hand edge of the photograph. This was a 104-gun first-rate ship of the line that had originally been launched at Portsmouth in 1825. Serving with the Mediterranean fleet between 1837 and 1841 and then in the West Indies, she was converted into a receiving hulk at Hong Kong in 1858 and was to fulfill that role until being sold in 1875. A receiving hulk was a vessel that was deemed no longer seaworthy but which was used primarily to house newly-recruited sailors prior to assignment to a specific ship; in places like Hong Kong they also served as floating hospitals and HMS *Princess Charlotte* was one of a number of redundant warships used for this purpose prior to the construction of the new Royal Naval Hospital at Wanchai in the 1870s. *Wellcome Foundation*

Constructed between the 1840s and 1874, Victoria Barracks comprised one of the most important British military bases on Hong Kong Island and was situated in an area bounded by Cotton Tree Drive, Kennedy Road and Queensway in Central. In 1868 – shortly before the date of this photograph (1870) – five accommodation blocks - 'A', 'B', 'C', 'D' and 'E' – were completed to house the Indian troops then used to garrison the colony; over the next century these buildings were used for a variety of purposes, including providing accommodation for the Gurkhas during the 1970s. After World War 2, and the Japanese occupation, the barracks were restored. From the late 1960s onwards, as the British military presence was reduced and other facilities were developed, the land on which the barracks were built was gradually returned to the Hong Kong government. Whilst some historical structures were preserved, the bulk of the barracks – including the five accommodation blocks – were all demolished. Part of the site was subsequently developed into Hong Kong Park whilst the southern part was redeveloped to include the High Court, the Queensway government offices and Pacific Place. *Commons Media*

Recorded in about 1873 by William Pryor Floyd, this is the Club Germania Building in Wyndham Street with one of the two-storey houses – Nos 1-9 Pedder's Hill – seen behind it. The latter were constructed in 1865 and were to survive until demolished in 1917. The Club Germania – or German Club – was established by Germans resident in Hong Kong in 1859 and this impressive building, designed in a neo-Gothic style by Wilson & Salway, was opened on 2 February 1872. The facilities on offer included two billiard rooms, a reading room, a bar and a concert room. The club moved to larger premises in 1902 but, as a result of World War 1 (when, for obvious reasons, Germans were not favoured in Hong Kong), the newer building was taken over by St Joseph's College. Following the transfer of the Club Germania, the building illustrated here had a second career as a hotel or boarding house before being occupied by the Nippon Club. Prior to demolition it was known as College Chambers.
Wellcome Collection

Viewed looking towards the north-east this view records West Point in the early 1870s. Historically, maps of Hong Kong recorded three points – East (near the modern Excelsior Hotel), North Point (still in use today) and West Point – along the north shore of Hong Kong Island, although the terms East Point and West Point are now largely historic. West Point was the northernmost point on the western half of the island prior to land reclamation and was located effectively at the junction of Des Voeux Road West and Western Street. The contemporary caption for the image records the following: 'Two of the most important native institutions in the colony are given in this view - viz., the Chinese Hospital and the Chinese Theatre. The roof and belfry of the German Mission Church can be seen over the former, while just beyond the church lies a large open space, which the Government has wisely enclosed as a native recreation ground. This part of the ground is named Possession Point. The Theatre may be distinguished by the inscription on the nearest face, visible over the intervening houses. The total native population of Hong Kong is about 120,000 souls.' *Wellcome Collection*

Again taken by William Pryor Floyd in about 1873, this view from the east shows the coastline with early jetties. The buildings and jetties in the foreground relate to the works of Jardine, Matheson & Co at East Point, an enterprise that was established here in 1843. Much of the harbour seen in this view has been subjected to reclamation and, by the date of this photograph, the first major scheme – the Praya Reclamation Scheme of 1868–73 – had just been completed. Over the past 150 years the coastline of much of Hong Kong Island has shifted significantly to the north as a result of further schemes. Such has been the scale of reclamation on both sides of Victoria Harbour that, in 1996, the Protection of the Harbour Ordinance was passed to safeguard the harbour against future development.

Wellcome Collection

Although Douglas Castle is still extant – and now forms University Hall, one of the residential halls of University of Hong Kong– the current building is much larger than the structure originally constructed on the top of Pok Fu Lam hill between 1861 and 1867 for the Scottish trader Douglas Lapraik seen in this view taken by William Pryor Floyd shortly after its completion. As built, in a neo-Gothic style, the building included an octagonal penthouse bedroom that faced the sea so that its owner could see the shipping entering and leaving the harbour. Following Lapraik's return to Britain in 1866 the house passed to his nephew John Steward Lapraik. In 1894, John Douglas Steward, who inherited the house following the death of his father, John Steward Lapraik, sold the building to the French Mission – the Société des Missions étrangères de Paris – who used it as a refuge during the outbreak of bubonic plague that affected Hong Kong that year. The building – renamed Nazareth – was converted into a monastery and significantly extended; the work included the construction of a chapel and a printing house. The French Mission continued to occupy the building until 1954 – with the exception of the period of the Japanese occupation when it was requisitioned by the occupying forces – when, as a result of the reduction in its missionary work, the monastery was closed. The building was sold to the University of Hong Kong on 4 December 1954 and converted into a hall of residence. *Wellcome Collection*

With the clock tower constructed in 1862 in the background, this view of Pedder's Wharf was taken in about 1868 by William Pryor Floyd. The building on the corner of Pedder Street and Praya Central was completed in 1863 and was initially occupied by Dent & Co; a company that operated from three buildings at the junction. Following the collapse of Dent & Co in 1867, the westernmost one of the trio – on the corner itself – was acquired by Melchers & Co, a business that had been established in Hong Kong the previous year. At the time the building was described as 'One dwelling house containing Five Rooms on the first Floor and Six Rooms on the Second Floor, with Bath Rooms, Kitchens, Out Offices, &c. &c, with Gas and Water laid on, and a Godown below, capable of holding about 2,000 tons.' The original wharf, as seen here, was replaced in 1886 and effectively became landlocked following the reclamation scheme of 1890 to 1904 whilst the building occupied by Melchers & Co was replaced three years later. Today this point forms the junction between Pedder Street and Des Voeux Road Central and the site is occupied by the Landmark complex. *Wellcome Collection*

This image, viewed across the Murray Parade Ground, records the City Hall, as opened on 3 September 1869 by Prince Alfred, Duke of Edinburgh; the construction of the building was funded by public subscription and the foundation stone was laid on 23 February 1867 by the then Governor, Sir Richard MacDonnell. The original photograph was taken by William Pryor Floyd in 1873. The building included, in its western half, a theatre and other facilities included a library and museum as well as rooms for balls, receptions and meetings. By the early 1930s the condition of the building had deteriorated and, in 1933, the western part – including the Theatre Royal – was demolished to permit the construction of the new headquarters of the Hongkong & Shanghai Bank. The remainder of the building was demolished in 1936. *Wellcome Collection*

When recorded by John Thomson in about 1870, Queen's Road East was a typical colonial street; the contrast with the view less than a century later (see 70) is dramatic. The Scottish-born John Thomson was a pioneer of travel photography and was one of the first photographers to venture to the Far East. He first travelled to Singapore in 1862 and travelled extensively through Malaysia, India and Sri Lanka as well as Cambodia and Vietnam. After a year back in Britain, he returned to the Far East in 1867 before settling in Hong Kong in 1868. He established a photographic studio in the Commercial Bank building, from where he recorded many views of Hong Kong whilst also using it as a base for his extensive travels to mainland China. He finally left the Far East to return to Britain in 1872. *Wellcome Collection*

A view taken in about 1870 by John Thomson from a high point on Murray Battery looking towards the west with Queen's Road in the centre. The building with the two towers on the centre-left of the image is the first Roman Catholic cathedral. The cathedral was opened on 22 June 1843 and, as can be seen, was a prominent structure that stood on the east side of Pottinger Street between Wellington Street and Hollywood Road. The cathedral was sold in 1881 but remained in use for a number of years whilst the later cathedral – see page 25 – was completed. The building was demolished in late 1886. Prominent on the north side of Queen's Road is the Hongkong Hotel; this was virtually brand-new when recorded here – it opened in 1868 – and was to survive in part until after World War 2. The northern wing of the hotel was destroyed by fire in 1926 and not rebuilt whilst the remainder was demolished in the 1950s with Central Building constructed on its site. Immediately to the west of the hotel can be seen the clock tower erected at the top of Pedder Street – see page 40. *Wellcome Collection*

Viewed looking south-west across the Botanical Gardens from Government House is The Albany. This was one of the earliest buildings to be constructed by the British on Hong Kong Island and dated originally to the late 1840s. Constructed as part of the Albany Barracks, named after the Duke of Albany, the complex passed to the government in the late 1850s before The Albany was sold to Charles May, who had just retired as Captain Superintendent of Police, in 1862. The house was to remain in the May family until it was sold in mid-1934 for HK$187,775. The building was demolished the following year and the site is now occupied by a children's playground alongside Robinson Road. The Hong Kong Zoological and Botanical Gardens – the oldest park in Hong Kong – were first established in 1864 and first opened to the public seven years later; as such it was one of the first such establishments in the world. *Wellcome Collection*

Situated on Staunton Street, the Union Church represented the second church occupied by the congregation, replacing one on Hollywood Road that had dated originally to 1845 and was founded by the London Missionary Society. The new church was completed in 1865 on the site of the old St Andrew's College but was destined to have a relatively short life as, in 1889, the land was acquired by the Hong Kong Land Investment Agency Co Ltd. The church was dismantled stone-by-stone and re-erected on Kennedy Road. For a period of time – until the new church opened on 11 January 1891 – the congregation held its services in the old City Hall (see page 17). The rebuilt church was demolished during the period of the Japanese occupation and a replacement church completed post-war. Although the post-war church was listed by the Antiquities and Monuments Office as a Grade III historic building, permission was granted in 2017 for its demolition and replacement with a 22-storey block that incorporated a new church as well as apartments. *Wellcome Collection*

Viewed from the south-east across Causeway Bay – long before the process of land reclamation saw the southern part of Causeway Bay converted into Victoria Park during the 1950s – is the sugar refinery established at East Point. This was established as Wahee Smith & Co in about 1874 but the owners were soon in financial trouble and the business was sold to Jardine Matheson & Co as the China Sugar Refining Co. The new owners constructed a wharf to facilitate the importation of raw sugar from China, Java, Malacca (part of the British Straits Settlements) and from The Philippines whilst processed sugar was shipped to China and India. Alongside the East Point refinery the company also possessed a distillery for the production of gin that was created from the byproducts of the sugar refining process. The sugar refinery and distillery were demolished in 1928. The area to the north of the long-demolished factory is now dominated by Victoria Park Road, which was completed in 1972, whilst the site of the factory is now, on the west side of Gloucester Road, occupied by retail and residential developments.
Wellcome Collection

Between 1877 and 1879 the former president of the United States of America, Ulysses S. Grant, undertook a prolonged world tour that saw him travel widely through Europe and East Asia. The tour, which saw him meet with a number of the most significant people including the then Pope, Leo XIII, the German Chancellor Otto von Bismarck and Queen Victoria, was part vacation and part diplomatic mission. As a result he was often conveyed by vessels of the US Navy and one of the consequences of the trip was the realisation that the USA was becoming a significant force on the world stage. In 1879, following his visit to India, Burma, Siam (Thailand), Singapore and Cochinchina (Vietnam), Grant and his wife visited Hong Kong and, to mark his visit, this decorative welcome arch was erected for him; it was recorded here on 16 May 1879. After his visit to Hong Kong, his group made its way to Canton, Shanghai and Beijing before reaching Japan. This was to be the last country visited on the tour prior to returning to the USA in September 1879. *Library of Congress*

This view, taken in the mid-1890s, records Cochrane Street looking towards the south from Queen's Road Central. There are a variety of traders visible – including a photographer's shop – as a hand cart is propelled westwards. Today, whilst Cochrane Street is still extant this view is now dominated by the presence of the Central Mid-Levels Escalator that ascends Cochrane Street at first-floor level. *Library of Congress*

Recorded here, viewed from the south-east, early in the 20th century shortly after completion, the Cathedral of the Immaculate Conception was the second to serve the Roman Catholic community on Hong Kong Island. The original cathedral, situated on Wellington Street, had been destroyed by fire with work commencing on its neo-Gothic replacement in 1883. The new building, situated by the Glenealy Ravine above Caine Road, was designed by the London-based architects Crawley & Co. The new cathedral opened on 7 December 1888; it was, however, not formally consecrated (as a result of the indebtedness incurred in its construction) until 8 December 1938. Slightly damaged during World War 2 – but protected from the worst ravages of the occupying forces as a result of its administration as part of the Pontifical Institute for Foreign Missions (based in Rome) as the Japanese were not at war with Italy – post-war the Cathedral has undergone significant changes. The original wooden roof was seriously damaged by termites and so was replaced by a concrete structure in 1952; this itself underwent significant repair as part of a major restoration scheme between 1997 and 2002. The cathedral has also seen a three-arched porch attached to its southern façade and the building is now surrounded by high-rise buildings that overshadow the now Grade I listed structure. *Library of Congress*

In 1887, at the time of the Golden Jubilee of Queen Victoria, it was decided to erect a statue to mark her reign. Although the statue itself was procured, a suitable location was not immediately available until land reclamation was completed. As a result it was not until 28 May 1896 that the then Governor, Sir William Robinson, formally unveiled the statue in Statue Square. The bronze sculpture was designed by the Italian-born but London-based artist Mario Raggi and cast in 1891 by the noted company of H. Young & Co in Pimlico, London, before being shipped out to Hong Kong. The new statue was situated under a canopy constructed from stone shipped from the famous Portland quarries in England. The surrounding iron railings were added in 1898.

Following the Japanese occupation of Hong Kong in World War 2, the statue – along with others – was shipped to Japan for melting down; fortunately, however, despite suffering some damage, the statue was recovered after the end of the war and shipped back to Hong Kong in October 1946 on board the *Fort Rosalie*. Following restoration, the statue of Victoria – now without its Portland stone canopy – was unveiled in a new location – Victoria Park – where it is still extant. *Library of Congress*

The Hong Kong Club was first established in 1846. Its original premises were situated on Queen's Road between D'Aguilar Street and Wyndham Street. Towards the end of the 19th century the club relocated to its present site on Jackson Road when it was granted a 999-year lease on 16 February 1895. The club employed the locally based architects Palmer & Turner to design its new building, which was completed in 1897 and is seen from the north-east in this view which must postdate 1923 as the newly constructed cenotaph can be seen in front of the structure. During the 1970s there were several proposals – rejected initially – for the demolition of the historic building and for the redevelopment of the site. In 1979 the club committee – despite concerted efforts by conservationists and appeals for the building's preservation that reached the then Governor Murray MacLehose – gave the go-ahead for the redevelopment of the site. By this date, the building represented one of the few surviving structures from the late 19th century on Hong Kong Island but this was not enough to ensure its survival. It was demolished in June 1981 and a 21-storey new club building, designed by Harry Seidler, was erected in its place. *Library of Congress*

With the statue erected to Queen Victoria on the right, this view across toward Statue Square sees the then newly constructed Supreme Court building. Designed by the well-known British architects Sir Aston Webb and Ingress Bell, work commenced on the construction of the court in 1900 and it was formally opened by the then Governor, Sir Frederick Lugard, on 15 January 1912. Built on reclaimed land, the foundations of the neo-classical building were formed by driving a large number of Chinese fir trees into the ground. The two-storey building occupies about 2,660sqm and the top of the dome reaches about 40m above ground level. The pediment facing Statue Square is surmounted by a statue of the Greek goddess of justice, Themis, which is based upon that which adorns the Old Bailey in London. Within the pediment itself is carved the royal coat of arms with figures depicting truth and mercy to the sides.

Following the transfer of legal work away from the building, the result of damage incurred during the construction of the MTR, the building was restored and was then used to house the Legislative Council of Hong Kong from 1985 until 2012 and, in 2015, reverted to legal work when it became the new seat of the Court of Final Appeal. *Library of Congress*

Recorded in about 1901, this view of the neo-classical Queen's Building records the four-storey office block shortly after its completion in 1899. The building was developed by Chater & Mody, a partnership that dated back to 1868, and was completed to the design of Leigh & Orange, an architectural practice established in Hong Kong in 1874, on reclaimed land. Regarded as amongst the most prestigious office accommodation in Central, the building had 16 office suites and amongst the tenants were the consulates of Denmark, Norway and Russia. The building was managed by Hong Kong Land from opening and was formally acquired by the company during the 1920s. It was demolished in the early 1960s with the Mandarin Oriental opening on the site in October 1963. The Praya Reclamation Scheme was a government project, first introduced in the 1880s, to increase the amount of available land for construction. Despite problems caused by lack of finance and the weather, the $3 million project was completed in 1904 and added 26 hectares of land for development. *Library of Congress*

The origins of the Central Market date back to the early 1840s and the establishment of the Canton Bazaar on Queen's Road Central between Cochrane Street and Graham Street. It was later moved to Queensway before a final move saw it relocated to Des Voeux Road in the 1850s. Rebuilt in 1858, by which date it had become known as the Central market, the structure was again to be rebuilt – in 1895 – to the three-storey neo-Classical building seen in this view taken in around 1900. Built in brick and granite, the upper floor was used for the supply of meat, poultry, fruit and game (when in season) whilst the lower for wholesalers and for fish and vegetables. A guide to Hong Kong published in 1895 claimed that 'The place is kept nice and clean and should be of interest to every visitor who may respect one of the most important of our sanitary and hygienic institutions'. This building itself was only to last until 1937 when it was demolished to be replaced by the present building that was formally opened on 1 May 1939. The new building, constructed in concrete in the Bauhaus style is a Grade III listed structure but is largely unused at the time of writing. *Library of Congress*

Soldiers of the 22nd Bombay Infantry regiment seen on parade in Kowloon in 1902. The regiment, which had been established originally as the 2nd Battalion of the 11th Regiment of Bombay Native Infantry in 1818, was known as the 22nd Bombay Infantry for a relatively brief period from 1901 until 1903 when it became the 122nd Rajputana Infantry. *Library of Congress*

Throughout the period of British occupation, the Royal Navy was a significant presence in Hong Kong. This view records some of the crew of HMS *Terrible* posed on the ship's forecastle. HMS *Terrible* was one of two 'Powerful' class cruisers built in response to a perceived threat from the Russian Navy's long-range armoured cruiser *Rurik*. *Terrible* was built on the River Clyde by J. & G. Thomson and was commissioned in 1898. Destined for the Royal Navy's China Station, *Terrible* was sent to the Far East via Simonstown in South Africa where the ship's guns were removed and attached to railway wagons for use during the Boer War, where they achieved fame in being used during the siege of Ladysmith. *Terrible* first arrived in Hong Kong in May 1900 and the cruiser's first action thereafter was in connection with the British military response to the Boxer Rebellion. At the time that the cruiser was recorded here, the ship was based in Hong Kong in order to provide relief and water for the naval dockyard at a time when the colony was being hit by a cholera epidemic. *Terrible* was to depart in July 1902 for home waters; she was to revisit Hong Kong periodically thereafter but was due for disposal in 1914. However, reprieved due to outbreak of World War 1, she completed her career as an engineering hulk in 1919 before being scrapped in 1932. *Library of Congress*

The Parsi cemetery in Hong Kong – recorded here in 1902 – was one of three established in the region by the Zoroastrian Charity Funds of Hongkong, Canton and Macao and is now the only one of the trio still functioning. The trust was established in Macao in 1822, to be followed by that in Guangzhou in 1834 and that in Hong Kong in 1852. Members of the Zoroastrian faith, many of whom were born in India, were drawn to Hong Kong during the 19th century by business opportunities. Amongst the most prominent was Sir Hormusjee Naorojee Mody, who, having been born in Bombay (Mumbai) in 1834 moved to Hong Kong in 1858 and helped establish the brokerage company Chater & Mody and was also to contribute significantly to the funding of University of Hong Kong. Another was Dorabjee Naorajee Mithaiwala, who came to Hong Kong in 1852 and was the founder of the Kowloon Ferry Co – later the Star Ferry – in 1888. Situated alongside other cemeteries in Happy Valley, there are now some 150 graves in the cemetery. *Library of Congress*

Horse racing was first introduced to Hong Kong following the establishment of the course in Happy Valley in 1845. The location, which required draining as it was previously largely swampland, was the only significant area of flat land before the process of land reclamation commenced. Following the construction of the course, the first races were actually held in December 1846. Initially racing was held once a year, normally to coincide with the Lunar New Year but the frequency of racing was increased. In order to regulate racing better the Hong Kong Jockey Club was established in 1884. This view records the running of the Hong Kong Derby in March 1902. The race was first run in 1873 and was to be a feature of the Happy Valley course for more than a century before it was transferred to the newer course at Sha Tin in 1979. The somewhat basic facilities seen in this view were to expand over the years but, in 1918, tragedy occurred when a fire swept through a temporary grandstand, resulting in the death of some 590 people. The racecourse is still active today albeit radically different to that more than a century ago and the backdrop is now one of skyscrapers rather than hillsides. *Library of Congress*

Taken in about 1903, this view records the entrance to the Royal Naval Hospital on Queen's Road East. The first seamen's hospital had been established in 1843 by Dr Peter Young of the East India Company but, by the 1870s, was making a loss and was acquired in 1873 by the Royal Navy to establish the navy's first permanent onshore hospital and relocated to the Mount Shadwell site illustrated here. The purchase and establishment of the new hospital was partly funded by the sale of a redundant warship – HMS *Melville* (a 74-gun third-rate ship of the line) – that had been used as a hospital ship since 1857. Over the years the facility was to grow significantly but was to be severely damaged during the war and, in 1949, was to become the Ruttonjee Sanatorium, the first hospital in Hong Kong to specialise in conditions such as tuberculosis and other heart and chest conditions. The work was supported by Jehangir Hormusjee Ruttonjee, another of the important Parsi community in Hong Kong at the time, in memory of his daughter, who had died of tuberculosis in 1941. The original hospital was demolished in 1991 and replaced by the new Ruttonjee Hospital, a 600-bed general hospital serving the Wan Chai district. *Library of Congress*

As a single-deck tram heads eastbound into Des Voeux Road, it passes the Alexandra Building at the junction with Chater Road. The building – nicknamed the 'Flat Iron' as a result of its shape – was constructed between 1901 and 1904 to a design of the architects Palmer & Turner on behalf of the Hong Kong Land Co, which had acquired the plot in December 1901. The ground floor was occupied by a number of retailers with the upper four floors being offices. The *South China Morning Post* described the building on completion: 'The building is surrounded by open verandahs designed in a restrained style of Renaissance. The lower storey has large arches standing on a granite base of the Doric order. The upper storeys have two simple orders crowned by a colonnade and principal cornice, above which rise small octagonal turrets enclosing a pleasing arcade of small arches topped by the plain steep gable ends of the roof. The corner of the building is carried up more than 135 feet above the street level with an open dome-capped colonnade rising above the steep conical roof.' The structure, which was originally known as the Alexandra Buildings (although the 'S' was soon dropped), was named after Queen Alexandra, wife of King Edward VII. It was demolished in 1952 and replaced by a second building of the same name; this, in turn, was demolished in 1974 and replaced by the current building. *Barry Cross Collection/Online Transport Archive*

In the late 19th century there were a number of proposals for the construction of tramways on Hong Kong Island. Of these plans, the only one to come to fruition initially was that proposed by the High Level Tramway Co and Alexander Findlay Smith – the Peak Tramway. The 848-yard long line from Garden Road to Victoria Gap was opened by Sir George William des Voeux, the then Governor, on 28 May 1888 following three years of construction. This view shows the lower – Garden Road – terminus from the south and shows to good effect the cable used to operate the funicular. When opened in 1888,

the power to operate the cable was generated by steam; this was replaced by electricity in 1926. The original cars were divided into three classes: First Class passengers were residents of Victoria Peak and British colonial officers; Second Class were members of the Hong Kong Police and the British armed forces; whilst the Third Class covered the remainder. Although the Peak Tramway remains open, the Garden Road terminus is radically different to the view seen here and the once sylvan backdrop has been replaced by modern buildings. *Barry Cross Collection/Online Transport Archive*

Above: The original Peak Hotel served the upper terminus of the Peak Tramway and opened with the funicular in 1888. This original hotel was provided with a bar, restaurant and some 20 bedrooms but was to be relatively short-lived as the then owner, Alexander Findlay Smith, capitalised on the new tramway and sold out. The new owners demolished the original hotel and constructed a new three-storey structure that opened in 1890. Over the years the hotel was extended significantly – as illustrated in this view taken in about 1920. In 1922 the Peak Hotel was again sold, for HK$600,000, but was to close in 1936. Following a fire two years later, the entire building was demolished. *Library of Congress*

Right: Taken in the early 1920s, when the P&O Building was under construction – it was completed in 1924 – this view records the General Post Office that was situated on the corner of Pedder Street and Connaught Road. By the late 19th century the existing buildings occupied by the various government departments were proving inadequate and plans for the construction of new buildings were formulated. The development of the GPO building started with the purchase of the site in 1902. Three designs for the building were received; that of Denison, Ram & Gibbs being accepted. Building work, however, was protracted as the scale of the building was altered whilst the foundations were under construction and it was not until 1911 that the building was finally completed. The prestigious building was completed in brick and granite with roof tiles supported on hardwood rafters. The P&O building alongside was to survive until 1961 and the GPO building itself was to be demolished in 1977. The site of the building was used to construct the then Pedder (later renamed Central) terminus of the MTR's Island Line and the World Wide House was subsequently constructed on the reclaimed land. *Library of Congress*

Recorded in about 1910, this view shows the clock tower that was situated at the southern end of Pedder Street towards its junction with Queen's Road Central. The image can be dated to that era as, on the right of the photograph, is the newly opened Jardine House – this was completed in 1909 – whilst the clock tower itself was to be demolished in 1913. The clock tower, which was 24m in height, was designed by a Mr Rawlings, and was to have been funded by public subscription; however, sufficient funds were not forthcoming until it was backed by Douglas Lapraik. Lapraik had been born in Scotland but arrived from Macao to Hong Kong in 1842. A watchmaker by trade, his personal fortunes increased when he co-founded the Whampoa Dock Company with Thomas Sutherland and Jardine, Matheson & Co in 1863. The clock tower itself was completed late the previous year and its chimes were heard for the first time on 31 December 1862. The Jardine Matheson Building was to survive until it was demolished in the mid-1950s. Its site is now occupied by Central Building. *Library of Congress*

In 1910, the government sold the original pier that was located adjacent to the General Post Office – seen on the extreme left of this view looking towards the west – and the rights to construct a new pier to the Star Ferry Co; the company had previously leased the earlier pier and had used it exclusively from 1900. The opening of the Kowloon Canton Railway and the expectation of increased traffic were factors in the decision to construct a new facility. Work commenced on the construction of the new pier in 1911 and work was completed the following year; this photograph was taken when the structure was relatively new. The gradual process of land reclamation resulted in the closure of the pier and its demolition in 1957 and the construction of a third pier slightly to the north; this itself was to fall victim to further reclamation in 2006 when it and the other ferry terminals were relocated to the waterfront adjacent to Man Kwong Street. *Library of Congress*

Above left: Believed to have been taken shortly after the end of World War 1, this view of a junk records HMS *Tamar* in the background. The Royal Navy vessel – the fourth to bear the name – was constructed on the River Thames, in London, and launched in June 1863. The 3,650 ton vessel was designed as a troopship and was fitted for both steam and sail power. She commenced her maiden voyage on 12 January 1864 sailing from the UK via Cape Town to the Far East. Following a 34-year career that saw her involved in actions off West Africa and Egypt, HMS *Tamar* became the Royal Navy's base ship in Hong Kong in 1897 and gave her name to the Royal Navy's shore station that was to be developed on the north coast of Hong Kong Island. Permanently moored in the harbour, HMS *Tamar* was to survive until being scuttled on 12 December 1941 during the Japanese attack upon Hong Kong in order to prevent the ship falling into enemy hands. Due to an airlock, the ship refused to sink with the result that, ultimately, she was sent to the bottom with the assistance of the Royal Artillery. It is believed that the remains of the scuttled ship were found during work in connection with the construction of the Central-Wan Chai bypass in 2014. *Library of Congress*

Above right: The statue of Queen Victoria in Statue Square is seen again with the Hong Kong Club in the background. The photograph can be dated to post 1923 as the Cenotaph is now present. *Library of Congress*

Mountain Lodge on Victoria Peak was the summer residence of the British Governor of Hong Kong for almost 80 years. The building illustrated in this 1931 view was the second structure on the site and was originally completed in 1900. Following the completion of a path from what is now known as Robinson Road – named after Hercules Robinson who was Governor from 1859 until 1865 – a military sanatorium was opened in 1862. This was, however, unsuccessful and did not last long. In 1867, Richard Graves MacDonnell, Governor from 1866 to 1872, purchased the site from the War Department and built the first Mountain Lodge. The original building suffered regularly from typhoon damage and had to be repaired on several occasions. By the end of the 19th century the building's condition had deteriorated significantly and the then Director of Public Works, Francis Cooper, was commissioned with its restoration. However, this proved impractical and the building was demolished. In 1898 Henry Arthur Blake was appointed Governor – he held the position to 1903 – and he commissioned Palmer & Turner to design the lodge illustrated here. The two-storey structure, designed in a neo-Renaissance style, was completed in 1902. In the late 1930s there were proposals for the construction of a new structure to replace both Government House and Mountain Lodge but these had not been developed before the Japanese occupation. In 1946, following the restoration of British rule, Mountain Lodge was demolished. In 1969 the site was developed as the Victoria Peak Garden; of the historic building, the Gate Lodge, also completed in 1902, on Mount Austin Road remains intact. *Library of Congress*

A view Hong Kong Harbour, taken in about November 1936 from Victoria Peak (when naval presence was increased in the region as a result of Japanese aggression in China), with ships of the Royal, French and US navies. Ships are: in the most distant offshore row (left to right): French light cruiser *Lamotte-Picquet*, Royal Navy submarine tender HMS *Medway* with several submarines alongside, and Royal Navy aircraft carrier HMS *Hermes*. In the nearest offshore row (left to right) are two destroyers (unidentified nationality), a French colonial sloop, USS *Augusta* and USS *Black Hawk* with two destroyers alongside. Alongside dockyard wharfs (left to right) are Royal Navy heavy cruiser HMS *Berwick* with two or three destroyers outboard, and Royal Navy heavy cruiser HMS *Cumberland*. Inside the dockyard basin (clockwise from entrance) are two destroyers, three submarines and an 'Insect' class gunboat. Offshore of, and to the right of, the dockyard (left to right) are USS *Isabel* alongside a US destroyer, two Royal Navy destroyers and six US destroyers. HMS *Cumberland* served on the Royal Navy's China station between 1928 and 1938 before being transferred to the South Atlantic; the 'County' class cruiser, which had been commissioned on 23 February 1928, was to achieve fame during World War 2 as one of the RN vessels involved in the later stages of the Battle of the River Plate in late 1939, an engagement that led to the scuttling of the German pocket battleship *Graf Spee*. She was to survive long enough to portray herself in the feature film *The Battle of the River Plate* in 1956. *US Navy/via Commons Media*

From the early years of the 20th century, as traffic levels increased, so too did the need for traffic control. In order to provide some shade for the police officers undertaking point duty at busy intersections shelters were constructed; these were initially quite basic, but by the 1950s a more sophisticated design had emerged – such as this example seen in 1956. Note the somewhat understated arrows around the base of the structure to indicate direction of travel and the cable from the roof to provide electric power for illumination. The design of the traffic pagodas was undertaken by Arthur May and the structures incorporated an insulated roof and, in some cases, a fan embedded in the base to counter the prevailing heat. The completed structure was just under 13ft in height.
Douglas Beath/Online Transport Archive

The Causeway Bay area recorded in 1956 sees the shacks of squatters on the hillside above the then new buildings. The lack of traffic – apart from the trams heading westbound along Causeway Road – is notable. Today, standing in a similar position, whilst the trams and road are constant factors, the backdrop is now dominated by modern high-rise buildings. *W. J. Wyse/LRTA (London Area) Collection/Online Transport Archive*

When the tramway was first constructed along Des Vœux Road Central, the traction columns carrying the overhead were placed – as seen in this view taken in the late summer of 1956 – in the centre of the road. As traffic increased, this arrangement was increasingly problematic and as a result work was undertaken between August and December that year to see the traction columns removed.
Douglas Beath/Online Transport Archive

Work is in progress during the autumn of 1956 on the reconstruction of the tramway along Des Voeux Road Central. With the traction columns removed, the overhead was now attached – not always with permission – to the buildings that ran alongside the road and the opportunity was taken to reduce the gap between the running lines. This work was to facilitate the construction of the loading islands along the road, a factor that enabled passengers to board and leave the trams more safely than previously. More than 60 years after the photograph was taken, although Des Voeux Road remains a relatively narrow thoroughfare – albeit now much busier than it was in 1956 – as does the tramway, the modern streetscape is dominated by modern buildings. *Dennis Beath/Online Transport Archive*

Buses of the Royal Army Services Corps (RASC) and Royal Corps of Transport (RCT) are seen at the school adjacent to RAF Sek Kong (now Shek Kong Airfield) in June 1965 as pupils make their way to the classrooms. The significant British military presence in the territory at the time resulted in large numbers of families also living in the married and family quarters that the military provided. Work started on the airfield at RAF Sek Kong in 1938 but its completion was delayed until 1950 as a result of the Japanese occupation between 1941 and 1945. The airfield was one of a number operated by the RAF during the period of British control but was to cease being used by the RAF in 1996. Neither the RASC nor the RCT still survive either; following various reorganisations within the British Army, their functions are now carried out by the Royal Logistic Corps.
Douglas Beath/Online Transport Archive

Two of the China Motor Bus Company's fleet of traditional British half-cab double-deck buses – AC4752 and AC4753 – are seen at North Point in November 1965. Both of the buses were Guy Arab Vs fitted with bodies supplied by Metal Sections Ltd and, when recorded here, were almost brand new, having been delivered some three months earlier. CMB, as the operator was widely known, was first established in 1924 and for many years the company was the only one to operate bus services on Hong Kong Island. However, following complaints about the quality of its services, it lost its franchised operations in 1998. Latterly it was to operate a single non-franchised service linking the Government Offices in North Point with Island Place; this was to operate for the last time on 1 July 2015 bringing to an end some 90 years of public service. *Douglas Beath/Online Transport Archive*

Once a familiar sight at important road intersections this pagoda controlling traffic was situated at the intersection of Queen's Road East and Hennessy Road. In the background is the building that accommodated the police married quarters. The development of the new police headquarters, to replace the earlier Central Police Station, commenced in the early 1950s and the block illustrated here was completed later in the decade. The married quarters were demolished in September 1987 to facilitate the redevelopment of the police station with Arsenal House – now Arsenal House (East Wing) – constructed on the site; this was completed in 1990. The adjacent Arsenal House (West Wing) was completed seven years later.
Douglas Beath/Online Transport Archive

Following the construction of an experimental single-deck trailer car in 1964, 20 more were ordered from the British company Metal Sections Ltd. These were delivered in kit form and were completed by Hongkong Tramways Ltd at Sharp Street depot. No 2, the first of these to enter service (on Christmas Eve 1965), is recorded when brand new during late December 1965. All of the 20 were in service by the end of 1967 with the company itself constructing a final trailer – No 22 – in September that year. The last of the trailers were to be scrapped in 1982. *Douglas Beath/Online Transport Archive*

When recorded in late 1965, it was still possible to see the Kowloon peninsula in the distance across Victoria Harbour from Des Voeux Road West along Hill Road as trams made use of the Whitty Street loop. Today the view is dominated by the Hill Road flyover and the main Route 4 Connaught Road West flyover, which was completed in 1997. The site of the building on the extreme right is now occupied by the Hong Kong Plaza. *Harry Luff/Online Transport Archive*

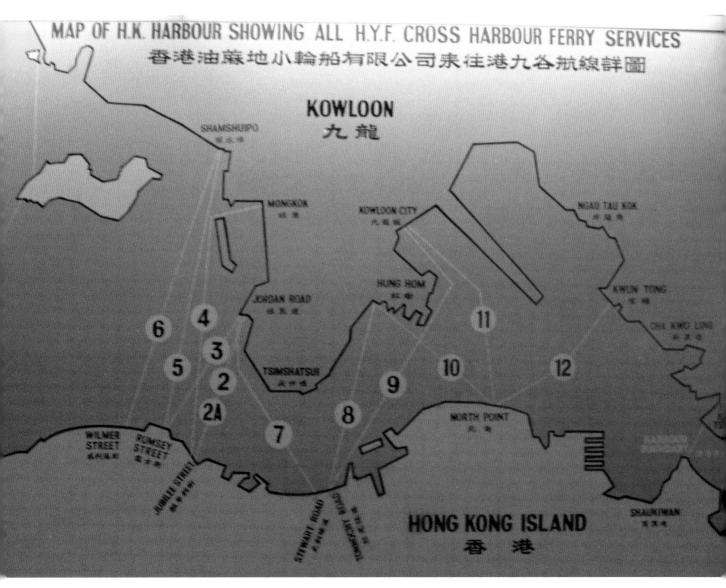

MAP OF H.K. HARBOUR SHOWING ALL H.Y.F. CROSS HARBOUR FERRY SERVICES

香港油蔴地小輪船有限公司來往港九各航線詳圖

KOWLOON
九龍

A map of the ferry services then in operation across Victoria Harbour as displayed in the Central Ferry Terminal in 1966. With the opening of the MTR and the completion of the three tunnels under the harbour (Cross Harbour in 1972, Eastern Harbour in 1989 and Western Harbour in 1997), the number of ferry services operating across the harbour from Hong Kong Island to the Kowloon Peninsula has been radically reduced. Today, Star Ferries provide links from Wan Chai and the Central Ferry Terminal to Tsim Sha Tsui. *Douglas Beath/Online Transport Archive*

Viewed across Victoria Harbour from Tsim Sha Tsui in 1966 as a ferry, one of the fleet then operated by the Hongkong & Yaumati Ferry Co (known as Hong Kong Ferry [Holdings] Co Ltd from 1989), disgorges its passengers, the skyline of Hong Kong Island is still relatively low rise. A similar view taken today would see the extent of development over the past 50 years with the International Finance Centre – stretching some 415m into the sky and thus making it the second tallest skyscraper in the SAR – now dominating the scene. *Douglas Beath/Online Transport Archive*

The Jordan Road ferry terminal recorded in 1966. From the 1920s there were plans to introduce a vehicular ferry service between Kowloon and Hong Kong Island and, in October 1930, plans for the construction of ferry terminals on Jordan Road, Kowloon, and Jubilee Street, Praya Central, were given. With work completed ferry services linking the two sides commenced in 1933. Alongside the Jordan Road terminal was the Jordan Road Ferry bus station; this was one of the oldest and largest bus stations in the territory and also commenced operation in 1933. In 1996, as a result of the West Kowloon Reclamation Project, the ferry terminal was moved to a temporary structure with the original building illustrated here being demolished. Two years later the ferry was withdrawn completely. Buses continued to serve the bus station until February 2003 when services were transferred to the Jordan (Wui Cheung Road) terminus with the site of the bus station now occupied by housing and by the MTR Austin station. *Douglas Beath/Online Transport Archive*

When Hong Kong Tramways commenced operation in 1904, the trams were housed in a small – 35-car – depot on Russell Street. This depot was enlarged in the 1920s in order to accommodate 90 trams but, by the early 1930s, even this depot was no longer sufficient and a second depot in North Point was added. In the early 1950s, with the modernisation of the tram fleet, the depot in North Point was closed and the main depot on Russell Street was further enlarged to accommodate both the entire operational fleet as well as the company's workshops. This view, taken from overhead in 1966, records the depot and workshops at a time when the tramcar fleet had increased to more than 160 cars in all. The Sharp Street facility was to serve the tramway for more than 30 years but was finally to close in 1989 and be replaced by new depots at Sai Wan Ho and Whitty Street. Following closure, the depot on Sharp Street was demolished and the site redeveloped. The site is now occupied by the Times Square shopping centre and office tower complex, which was opened in April 1994. *Douglas Beath/Online Transport Archive*

Above and opposite: Surviving until 1976, the iron ore mine at Ma On Shan, located a short distance from the village of Ma On Shan Tsuen in the New Territories, was the biggest to operate in Hong Kong. The site began its operations in 1906 when the Hong Kong Mining Corporation was granted a licence to explore for and extract iron ore from the site. Passing through various owners, the mine survived World War 2 and was considerably expanded in 1949. By the early 1950s, iron ore at the middle and upper levels was being exhausted and the then owners, the Mutual Mining & Trade Co, began mining underground and by the end of the decade all work was being undertaken underground. By 1963 the mine employed 650 people but, by the early 1970s, worldwide supply of iron ore exceeded demand and the mine finally closed, with the loss of 400 jobs. The mining licence finally expired in March 1981. During the mid 1960s the mine was operated by Kühn Mines Ltd and served by an extensive narrow-gauge electric powered railway. This and the next two views, all taken during a visit to the mines in 1966, provide a reminder of the operation of this once important mine and the railways that once served it.

Douglas Beath/Online Transport Archive (all)

With Pedder Street and the old Post Office on the left, this is a view along Connaught Road looking towards the west in 1966. The ugly extension from the façade of the Post Office was designed to facilitate the loading and unloading of mailbags to and from ships moored at the quayside. In the 50 years since this view was taken land reclamation has seen the coast with its numerous ferry terminals moved some half-a-mile to the north. Apart from the replacement of the Post Office by World Wide House, Connaught Road has been significantly upgraded. In place of the overhead bridge connecting into the old Post Office there is now a pedestrian bridge linking World Wide House with Exchange Square and the whole backdrop is dominated by skyscrapers to either side of Connaught Road. *Douglas Beath/Online Transport Archive*

Viewed towards the north along Pedder Street, the Post Office of 1911 is on the left with, on the right, Union House. The latter was relatively new at this time – having been completed in 1962. Prior to the construction of the new building, the site had been occupied by three structures – the King's Building, the York Building and the Mansions (or Union) Building. The first two were demolished in 1958 to allow work on Phase 1 of the new structure to commence, with the Union Building following four years later. The replacement structure, which had 23 storeys, was renamed Swire House in 1976. Swire House itself was demolished in 1998 and the new Chater House was completed on the site in 2002. Beyond the T-junction with Connaught Road can be seen the site of the original Blake Pier; by this date the pier, which was originally opened in 1900, had been demolished as part of Phase 1 of the Central Area Reclamation Scheme. *Douglas Beath/Online Transport Archive*

In 1962 the original Prince's Building was demolished and the second building to bear the name was built to the design of the architects Palmer & Turner. This view, looking to the west along Chater Road in 1966, sees the new Prince's Building shortly after its completion linked by a footbridge to the Mandarin Hotel. The hotel was constructed on the site of the old Queen's Building – see page 29 – and was completed in 1963. The hotel was designed by John Leigh of the architects Leigh & Orange and, when completed with its 26 storeys, was the tallest building then erected in Hong Kong; this was a record that it was not to hold for long. Although both the second Prince's Building and the Mandarin Hotel – known as the Mandarin Oriental since 1985 – are both still extant, as is the footbridge, both buildings have undergone refurbishment since the date of this photograph. The hotel underwent a multi-million dollar renovation, which resulted in its temporary closure between December 2005 and September 2006. *Douglas Beath/Online Transport Archive*

With Star House under construction on the left, this view of the Tsim Sha Tsui Star Ferry terminal and the old station that served the Kowloon Canton Railway was taken from the north-west in 1966. The first pier to serve cross-harbour ferries here opened in 1906 but was destroyed by a typhoon later the same year. A new pier opened in 1914; this was to survive until the early 1950s when the present structure was constructed. This was completed in 1957. Kowloon railway station was opened as the railway's southern terminus on 1 October 1910. The new building included a two-storey building allied to a clock tower – the presence of the tower meant that the Star Ferry building did not have a clock unlike that constructed on Hong Kong Island – as well as a significant freight yard slightly to the north. The station – with the exception of the clock tower (which was preserved in situ with – eventually – its bell restored) – was demolished in 1978, following closure in 1974 and despite a strenuous local campaign for the building's preservation. The site of the station is now occupied by the Hong Kong Cultural Centre, which was finally opened by the Prince and Princess of Wales on 8 November 1989.
Douglas Beath/Online Transport Archive

Hong Kong bus operators were, historically, major customers for traditional British designed and built front-engined double-deck buses. This is a view taken in 1966 of the lower-deck interior of Kowloon Motor Bus D294 (AD5750), which was a Daimler CVG6/30 fitted with a body supplied by Metal Sections Ltd – the same company that built 20 of the trailer cars used on the tramway – that was new in 1962.
Douglas Beath/Online Transport Archive

Seating on the trams was relatively spartan until the fleet was modernised in the 1980s; this 1966 view of the upper deck of No 21 – new in 1951 – shows the standard wooden seating that was offered. At this stage the upper deck was reserved for first-class passengers, who entered the tram via the front entrance, whilst the lower deck was occupied by third-class passengers, who entered via the rear platform. The two-class fare structure was abolished in 1972. *Douglas Beath/Online Transport Archive*

Viewed looking towards the south with the race course at Happy Valley in the background, the ground occupied by the Hong Kong Football Club can be seen at the northern edge of the race course as a tram makes its way southbound along Morrison Hill Road. This view is now very different. Although the race course is still extant, the Wong Nai Chung Gap Flyover now passes above Morrison Hill Road just to the north of the sports facilities. The football ground seen here was the result of major rebuilding work in the 1950s when it was largely reconstructed in concrete. Work commenced in 1953 on the rebuilding of the North and South stands and the rebuilding work was complete for the start of the 1954/55 season in September 1954. The use of the floodlighting took place for the first time on 5 January 1955. By the 1970s, the concrete ground was starting to show its age and was completely rebuilt for the centenary of the football ground in 1986. However, the new ground was to last less than a decade with the Jockey Club funding the transfer of the football club to a new ground in 1995 within the actual race course circuit. Following demolition of the football ground, alternative sports facilities were provided whilst the Jockey Club also demolished its adjacent headquarters – constructed in 1951 – and replaced it with the fourth generation structure that stands on the site today. Although trams continue to ply their way along Morrison Hill Road, the buildings extant in 1966 have been swept away and the sites redeveloped.

Douglas Beath/Online Transport Archive

Passengers queue for taxis having just disembarked from the ferries at Blake Pier. When recorded here in 1966 the pier was new, having replaced the original Blake Pier (itself eventually relocated to Stanley), earlier in the decade. The pier was named after Sir Henry Arthur Blake, who was the Governor of Hong Kong between 1898 and 1903. The second generation Blake Pier was to be demolished in 1993 as part of Phase 1 of the Central Reclamation scheme.

With a policeman controlling traffic on Queen's Road East from one of the traditional pagodas on the extreme left, a tram makes its way eastbound along Queen's Road East past HMS *Tamar*, the Royal Navy's primary base in Hong Kong between 1897 and 1997. In the background is the three-storey structure that formed the Rodney Block of the Wellington Barracks. The origins of the barracks dated back to the establishment of a battery in 1842; from the early 1850s the site was known as Wellington Battery after the Duke of Wellington, who died in 1852. The site was one of a number developed by the British military in the Admiralty district following the reclamation of land. The presence of the military in Admiralty caused problems for the development of Hong Kong Island between Central and Wan Chai and, from the mid-1950s, the military was under pressure to release land for redevelopment. This was partially achieved through further land reclamation and the restructuring of the naval base. The site of Wellington Barracks was passed from the military to the Hong Kong government in the 1970s and was subsequently cleared. Today, the space is occupied by Harcourt Garden.
Douglas Beath/Online Transport Archive

Passengers await an eastbound tram at the shelter situated at the western end of Victoria Park on Causeway Road in 1967. Although the trams remain as a constant feature of the view from more than 50 years ago, the backdrop is radically different. No longer is it possible to see the hillside in the distance as modern skyscrapers – such as the Pak Lok Commercial Building and Park Towers – of Causeway Bay dominate the view whilst, in the foreground, the Gloucester Road flyover passes overhead. *Douglas Beath/Online Transport Archive*

During the 1950s the Peak Tramway underwent modernisation with three new cars – two in service with a third held as a spare – introduced in 1956. A decade later – on 3 March 1967 – one of the trio is seen on the steeply graded funicular. These cars, which could accommodate 62 passengers, were themselves destined to be replaced in 1989 by new Swiss-built cars, although one of the 1956-built cars was retained and is now displayed at the tramway's upper terminus. *Douglas Beath/Online Transport Archive*

Work is in progress in 1967 on the construction of the tram turning loop at the western end of Causeway Road at its intersection with Irving Street and Yee Wo Street. The loop was built to avoid the necessity of reversing the tramcars when making use of the crossover at the eastern end of Victoria Park. Today, although the tramway remains a common feature of the view, as does the footbridge across Irving Street, most of the buildings visible have been replaced. At the eastern end of Yee Wo Street, the building on the southern side has been replaced by the Regal Hong Kong Hotel and on the northern side by the Lok Sing Building A. *Douglas Beath/Online Transport Archive*

In 1961, the Kowloon Canton Railway acquired three new Co-Co diesel locomotives – Nos 56-58 – from General Motors' Electro-Motive Diesel Division in the USA. Five years later a fourth of the type – No 59 – was acquired; this time the locomotive was built by the Australian manufacturer Clyde Engineering under licence from General Motors. The quartet, designated as EMD G16s by the manufacturer, followed on from an earlier batch of General Motors-built locomotives Nos 51-55, which were designated G12 and delivered between 1954 and 1957. No 59 – seen here in the autumn of 1980 in KCR livery – was, like the other G16s, fitted with a 16-567C diesel engine; however, following a collision and rebuilding, the locomotive was subsequently fitted with a replacement 16-645E engine. All four of the G16s were to pass to the MTR following the merger with the KCR in 2007 but all are now withdrawn.

J. M. Jarvis/Online Transport Archive

With two ships from the Royal Navy – RFA *Blue Rover* and 'Leander' class frigate HMS *Naiad* – in the background, Star Ferry *Silver Star* approaches the terminal at Tsim Sha Tsui in the late summer of 1980. The ferry is one of the newest vessels in the Star Ferry fleet; it was completed by the Hong Kong & Whampoa Dock Co in 1965 and remains in service at the time of writing. RFA *Blue Rover* was built by Swan Hunter on the River Tyne in England and entered service with the Royal Fleet Auxiliary in 1970. One of the batch of five 'Rover' class tankers employed, it was sold to the Portuguese Navy in 1993. HMS *Naiad* (F39) was built on the River Clyde in Scotland by Yarrow & Co Ltd and commissioned in March 1965; the frigate was destined ultimately to be sunk as a target during an exercise in 1990.

J. M. Jarvis/Online Transport Archive

With the Sun Hung Kai Centre under construction in the foreground, this view taken towards the west in the autumn of 1980 shows the Wanchai district from Causeway Bay. Although the Sun Hang Kai Centre remains, although modified by the addition of a further five storeys added in 1991, more modern developments mean that the view of the Peak in the district is now largely obscured.
J. M. Jarvis/Online Transport Archive

When recorded here in 1981 looking towards the east, Praya Kennedy Town could legitimately make the claim that it was still adjacent to the harbour with the scene busy with myriad small vessels discharging assorted goods into the lorries on the adjacent quayside. Today this scene is radically different; although the tramway, with its central traction columns, is still present, land reclamation schemes have seen the coastline shifted some distance to the north with some of the reclaimed land used for the Belcher Bay Park and the Kennedy Town swimming pool. *Richard Lomas/Online Transport Archive*

The congested nature of Praya Kennedy Town is emphasised in this view, taken at the same time as the previous image but looking towards the west. Some 40 years after the photograph was taken, virtually the only constant feature of the view is the tramway.
Richard Lomas/Online Transport Archive

The development of Discovery Bay, on Lantau Island, was first proposed in the early 1970s with the establishment of the Hong Kong Resort Co but it was not until 1979 that construction work on the initial phases commenced. The first accommodation units to be occupied were completed in 1982 and, by the early 1990s, some six phases of the development – comprising a total of some 3,300 units in all – had been finished. This view, taken looking towards the east, records the scale of this private development in 1989; since this date a further nine phases have been constructed, adding a further 2,800 units. The population of Discovery Bay now totals in excess of 20,000 and the resort includes its own marina, golf course and man-made beach. In the future, it is likely that such a panoramic view across the harbour may disappear; in October 2018 a development plan was announced that would see some 1,700 hectares of land reclaimed from the sea primarily to the south and east of Peng Chau island, east of Lantau, as part of the Lantau Tomorrow Vision. If completed, it is estimated that some 1.5 million people will be accommodated on the new land. *Joan Waller*

A view across towards Tsim Sha Tsui from Hong Kong Island in late 1989 sees the clock tower of the former KCR station backed by the then recently completed Cultural Centre and, to the left, Star House. Although these structures, as well as the Star Ferry terminal, are still extant, the skyline of the Kowloon peninsula has radically altered over the past 30 years. *Joan Waller*

Following the demolition of the bulk of the former KCR terminus, the distinctive clock tower was left standing with the new Cultural Centre constructed where the bulk of the station had once stood. After some delays, partly the result of escalating costs, the Cultural Centre was officially opened on 8 November 1989 by the Prince and Princess of Wales. In this view, taken from the south-east, Star House – with its once familiar 'Motorola' legend along the skyline – can be seen in the background. This was built in 1966 and remains extant today, albeit now promoting a different company. As elsewhere, however, whilst the foreground may be very similar some 30 years after the photograph was taken, the skyline beyond Star House has changed with the construction of the International Commerce Centre, currently Hong Kong's tallest building at 484m, which was completed in 2010. *Joan Waller*

The view across Victoria Harbour in September 1992 shows the ever-changing skyline of Central in the foreground and Kowloon in the distance. Prominent toward to the east is the Bank of China Tower. Designed by I. M. Pei & Partners, the tower was built on the site of Murray House – a Victorian era building that was relocated to Stanley following its careful dismantling – between 1986 and 1989. When completed, the tower – at 1,033ft in height and with its masts reaching 1,205ft – was the tallest building in Hong Kong and was the first structure outside the United States to break the 1,000ft mark. It was to remain the tallest structure in Hong Kong until 1992. It was supplanted by Central Plaza – out of view to the east in Wan Chai in this shot – and by the Two International Finance Centre in Central and by the International Commerce Centre in Kowloon; these were completed in 2003 and 2010 respectively and now dominate the view from Victoria Peak along with other more modern high-rise buildings. In the distance, stretching into Kowloon Bay, can be seen Kai Tak airport with its extended runway. Following the completion of the new airport at Chek Lap Kok, Kai Tak was finally closed on 6 July 1998. *Author*

Recorded at Whitty Street on 23 September 1992 is a China Motor Bus single-deck service vehicle, registered AH4134. This had originally been a double-deck bus – M41 – which was a Guy Arab Mark V fitted with a 68-seat body when new originally in June 1971. When withdrawn 12 years later, it was converted into a single-decker that retained its lower-deck seating but was fitted with doors on both sides and, as such, was used as an engineering and logistical vehicle until final withdrawal. The registration is currently in use on a three-axle Citybus Volvo Super Olympian double-decker No 250 that had previously been operated by New World First Bus. *Author*

The Cenotaph in Hong Kong, pictured here in September 1992, was built under the auspices of the locally-based architectural practice of Palmer & Turner with its design based upon the cenotaph – literally 'empty tomb' – designed by the great British architect Sir Edwin Lutyens and erected in Whitehall, London, in 1920. The structure, inscribed with the words 'The Glorious Dead', was erected in tribute to all those who had made the supreme sacrifice in World War 1 and was formally unveiled by the then Governor, Sir Reginald Edward Stubbs. Following World War 2, the dates 1939-1945 were added. Prior to the transfer of Hong Kong in 1997, the cenotaph displayed – as that in London still does – the flag of the United Kingdom along with flags representing the country's armed forces on a daily basis. Since 1997, the only flags to be displayed – on Remembrance Day alone (when a memorial service is still held) – are those of the Hong Kong Ex-Servicemen's Association, the People's Republic of China and that of Hong Kong itself. *Author*

Now the official residence of the Chief Executive of Hong Kong, when recorded here in September 1992 Government House was still the official residence of the British Governor. The last person to hold this role was Chris Patten, who had been appointed to the position three months earlier. Government House was designed by Charles St George Cleverly, with construction commencing in 1851. The neoclassical building was completed four years later with Sir John Bowring being the first Governor to occupy it. Apart from acting as the Governor's residence, the building also accommodated the Legislative Council of Hong Kong between 1855 and the 1930s. Although the first Chief Executive of the SAR did not reside in Government House, his successor Donald Tsang did following a renovation project that cost some HK$14.5 million. *Author*

The fishing village of Tai O, situated on the west coast of Lantau Island is the point at which the Tai O River enters the South China Sea through two channels creating a smaller island on which the western half of the village is situated. The village itself is built primarily on stilts and the sections are now linked by two footbridges. In 1992, however, when this view was taken, the primary means of gaining access from Lantau Island to the smaller island was via this small rope-operated ferry. Although there is archaeological evidence for human activity around Tai O in the Stone Age and the Portuguese briefly occupied the area in the early 16th century, the modern village developed from a Tanka fishing community. Much of the area was destroyed by fire in 2000 but was subsequently rebuilt although fishing – the traditional trade – is now in almost terminal decline.
Author

The northernmost station on the Kowloon Canton Railway and the interchange point between Hong Kong and the People's Republic of China is Lo Wu. Pictured at the station in September 1992 is one of the EMUs built in Britain by Metro Cammell for the service on the line between 1982 and 1990. No E75 was one of the sets ordered in 1986. Between 1996 and 1999 the Metro Cammell-built units underwent a major refurbishment, designed to extend their lives; this work included rebuilt front ends and so the refurbished units looked radically different to the units as built. In 2012 replacement rolling stock was ordered from the South Korean manufacturer Hyundai Rotem and all of the Metro Cammell units are due for replacement by the end of 2020. *Author*

Taken in 1992 looking towards the north-east from Peng Chau Island, this view records shipping in the western approaches to Victoria Harbour with Tsing Yi Island and the peaks of the Kowloon peninsula beyond. The completion of the new airport at Chek Lap Kok resulted in the construction of a dual carriageway from Kowloon westwards. The new road crosses from Kowloon to Tsing Yi Island over the Stonecutters Bridge – a name that commemorates the island that was formerly used as a Royal Navy base but has now been joined to Kowloon by reclamation – and from Tsing Yi Island to Lantau over the Tsing Ma bridge. The southern end of Tsing Yi Island is now occupied by a number of oil depots whilst the coastline on the east of the island has been reclaimed and redeveloped as Kwai Tsing Container Terminal 9; this facility was finally opened on 22 July 2003. *Author*

Following the completion of the Praya East Reclamation in 1930, development of the reclaimed land commenced. Amongst the buildings to be constructed was the Chinese Methodist Church at the junction of Johnston Road and Hennessy Road. The church's foundation stone noted the date of the start of construction as 13 April 1935 and the new church was completed the following year. The Methodist congregation was first established in a building on Wellington Street in 1882, moving to Aberdeen Street and then Caine Road before moving to the new church on Hennessy Road. The building was a distinctive landmark, being triangular in shape and incorporating green glazed roof tiles. The building, seen here in 1992, was demolished during the summer of 1994 and a new 23-storey structure, incorporating a new church, was completed four years later. *Author*

Viewed looking towards the east from the reclaimed land on which the various ferry terminals serving Central stand, the Wan Chai district is recorded here in 1992. Although the skyline itself – dominated by the skyscrapers of the district – is largely unchanged more than a quarter of a century on, the foreground had been radically changed. Following completion of the first Convention and Exhibition Centre in 1988, a second facility – built on an artificial island situated in Victoria Harbour – was constructed between 1994 and 1997. The northernmost part of the artificial island is occupied by Golden Bauhinia Square, which is dominated by a six-metre sculpture of a bauhinia plant on top of a red granite pillar. *Author*

One of the familiar ships operated by the Star Ferry Co Ltd is seen departing for Kowloon on 23 September 1993. The *Meridian Star* was constructed by Hong Kong & Whampoa Dock at the company's shipyard in Kowloon in 1958. The ferry, which remains in service (as one of the oldest vessels in the fleet), was modified between 2012 and 2013 in order to operate as a back-up for the harbour tour operated by the company. The Edinburgh Place ferry pier was the third generation terminal operated on Hong Kong Island for Star Ferry services to Kowloon; largely designed by the local architect Hung Yip Chan of the government's architecture department (although the famous clock tower was added by the then Chief Architect, Malcolm Wright) and completed in 1957, the building was completed in the then popular Modernism style. The new structure, required as a result of land reclamation, was itself to fall victim to further redevelopment and was to be closed in November 2006 and – despite considerable opposition – was demolished the following month. Efforts to try and preserve the clock tower with its clock – the gift of John Keswick – came to nothing.

John Meredith/Online Transport Archive

Constructed in 1859, the old police station in Stanley is now the oldest surviving police station in Hong Kong. The building was extended during the Japanese occupation during World War 2 by the construction of a mortuary. After World War 2 the building remained in use as a police station until closure in 1974; declared a monument in 1984, the building has had a number of commercial uses and is, at the time of writing, occupied by a supermarket. Since this view was taken in 1993 the building, whilst substantially unaltered, has lost the flower boxes around the first floor balcony – making it look much starker – whilst the bus stop has been modified, including the loss of the barrier. *Author*

With work in the background that will radically alter this location for ever – the construction of the new airport at Chek Lap Kok – this view of the battery at Tung Chung, at the northern end of Lantau, is taken looking towards the north-east. The battery was originally constructed in 1817 in order to protect Tung Chung Bay from pirates. Lacking a navy at the time, the Chinese built a number of forts in order to defend its coastline. Lost for almost a century, the remains of the structure – this L-shaped wall with a corner platform designed to act as a gun emplacement – were rediscovered in 1980. Following restoration, the battery was declared a monument three years later.
Author

Situated in Tung Chung is the Hau Wong Temple dedicated to Yeung Hau, a court official who served the last emperor of the Song dynasty, Zhao Bing, who died in 1279. The temple itself was constructed in 1765. When recorded here in October 1993, the site was one of relative peace and quiet; today, although the temple itself is still extant – and has recently undergone renovation – the backdrop has radically altered. With the completion of the new airport, a new town – the first to be constructed on one of the outlying islands – was completed as part of the Airport Core Programme on reclaimed land on the north coast of Lantau Island. Work commenced on the project in the mid-1990s and, eventually, it is planned that the community will accommodate some 250,000. As a result the backdrop visible here has been replaced by the tower blocks of Tung Chung new town. *Author*

In the late 1980s the Peak Tramway underwent modernisation with two new trams supplied by the Swiss company Gangloff AG. Each of these vehicles could carry up to 120 passengers but, as traffic continued to increase, more capacity was required. As a result, in April 2019 the service was temporarily suspended whilst the line was again modernised and larger trams – with a capacity of up to 210 – introduced. Services were restored during the summer of 2019. In this view, taken during the spring of 1995, one of the 1989 cars can be seen passing under Cotton Tree Drive with the Helena May Institute – or The Helena May – visible in the background. The construction of this building – now a Declared Monument – was begun in 1914 and officially opened on 12 September 1916 by Helena May, the daughter of Lt-Gen George Digby Barker (the British military commander in China and Hong Kong between 1890 and 1895), for the use of unaccompanied women who had arrived in Hong Kong. Used by the Japanese during the war and by the Royal Air Force briefly after the Japanese defeat, the Helena May was to start admitting male members in 1985.

Alan Pearce/Online Transport Archive

The sun sets over Hong Kong on 1 November 1993 as Hong Kong Island and Victoria Peak are viewed across the harbour from Kowloon. In the three decades since this photograph was taken, much has changed in Hong Kong – and the skyline has considerably altered in the intervening period – but the essential dynamism and vibrancy of the place remains. Hong Kong was – and is – one of the greatest multi-cultural cities in the world; its ever-changing built environment is a testament to this inescapable fact. *Author*